animal babies

on mountains

KINGFISHER

Kingfisher Publications Plc
New Penderel House
283–288 High Holborn
London WC1V 7HZ
www.kingfisherpub.com

First published by Kingfisher Publications Plc 2005
10 9 8 7 6 5 4 3 2 1

1TR/0505/TWP/SGCH(SGCH)/150STORA/C

Copyright © Kingfisher Publications Plc 2005

A CIP catalogue record for this book is available from the British Library.

ISBN–13: 978 0 7534 1078 3
ISBN–10: 0 7534 1078 8

Author: Jennifer Schofield
Editor: Vicky Weber
Designer: Joanne Brown
Picture Manager: Cee Weston-Baker
Picture Researcher: Rachael Swann
DTP Manager: Nicky Studdart
Production Controller: Jessamy Oldfield

Printed in Singapore

animal babies

on mountains

I have thick, soft fur
to keep me warm.
When I am bigger,
I will grow a beard.

Who is my mummy?

My **mummy** is a
mountain goat and
I am her **kid**.

Our sharp **hooves** help
us **climb** steep, rocky
mountain slopes.

When I am young, I am small and fluffy. But as I grow up, I get much bigger and stronger.

Who is my mummy?

My **mummy** is a brown bear and I am her **cub**.

If I feel **afraid**, she **nuzzles** me with her soft, **warm** nose.

I have small hands with tiny claws. I use my hands to hold my food when I eat.

Who is my mummy?

My mummy is a marmot and I am her baby.

In the winter, we sleep under the ground in a warm burrow.

My fur is white
with black patches.
My favourite food
is bamboo.

Who is my mummy?

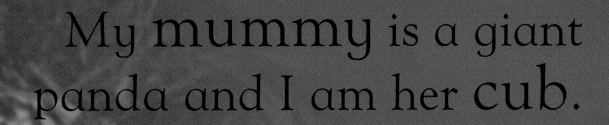

My **mummy** is a giant panda and I am her **cub**.

We **live** in China. Our home is in **bamboo forests**, high up in the mountains.

I have a long neck, and pointed ears. I can twist my ears around to listen out for danger.

Who is my mummy?

My mummy is
a llama and
I am her calf.

We can run very
quickly on our
long, thin legs.

In winter, my brown fur becomes very thick. It keeps me warm when it is cold.

Who is my mummy?

My **mummy** is a monkey and I am her **baby**.

We like to wash our **food** in the **river** before we eat.

I have small round
ears, a furry face
and whiskers –
just like a cat.

Who is my mummy?

My mummy is a snow leopard and I am her cub.

Our smoky grey fur has dark spots. It helps us hide amongst the trees.

Additional Information

The mountains throughout the world are teeming with a great variety of plant and animal life. Some of the animals found in this book, such as brown bears, venture into the mountains if they are unable to find adequate food supplies at lower altitudes; otherwise they live in lowland. Other animals featured, such as giant pandas, live permanently in the mountains as the climate and food supply of these lofty habitats suit their needs.

Acknowledgements

The publisher would like to thank the following for permission to reproduce their material. Every care has been taken to trace copyright holders. However, if there have been unintentional omissions or failure to trace copyright holders, we apologise and will, if informed, endeavour to make corrections in any future edition.

Cover: Alamy/Steve Bloom; Half title page: Oxford Scientific Films; Title page: Nature/Ingo Arndt; Mountain goat 1: Getty Images/Imagebank; Mountain goat 2: Oxford Scientific Films/Bob Bennett; Brown bear 1: Getty/John Eastcott and Yva Momatiuk; Brown bear 2: Getty/John Eastcott and Yva Momatiuk; Marmot 1: NHPA; Marmot 2: Ardea; Giant panda 1: Alamy/Steve Bloom; Giant panda 2: Alamy/Steve Bloom; Llama 1: Oxford Scientific Films; Llama 2: Alamy/Steve Bloom; Monkey 1: Corbis/Wolfgang Kaehler; Monkey 2: Corbis/Wolfgang Kaehler; Snow leopard 1: Getty/Keren Su; Snow leopard 2: Nature/Ingo Arndt